P9-DEL-717

GAIL BORDEN
Public Library District
200 No. Grove Avenue
Elgin, Illinois 60120
(847) 742-2411.

SPACE SHUTTLE

Published by Smart Apple Media

123 South Broad Street

Mankato, Minnesota 56001

Copyright © 2000 Smart Apple Media.

International copyright reserved in all countries. No part

of this book may be reproduced in any form without written

permission from the publisher.

Printed in the United States of America.

Photos: nasa/kennedy space center

Design and Production: EvansDay Design

Library of Congress Cataloging-in-Publication Data

Richardson, Adele, 1966–

Space shuttle / by Adele D. Richardson

p. cm. — (Above and beyond)

Includes index.

Summary: Examines the development and components of space

shuttles and how they have been used to explore outer space.

ISBN 1-58340-052-4

1. Space shuttles—Juvenile literature. [1. Space shuttles.

2. Outer space—Exploration.] I. Title. II. Series: Above

and beyond (Mankato, Minn.)

TL795.5.R53   1999

629.44'1'0973—DC21   98-41869

First edition

1 3 5 7 9 8 6 4 2

SPACE SHUTTLE

ADELE D. RICHARDSON

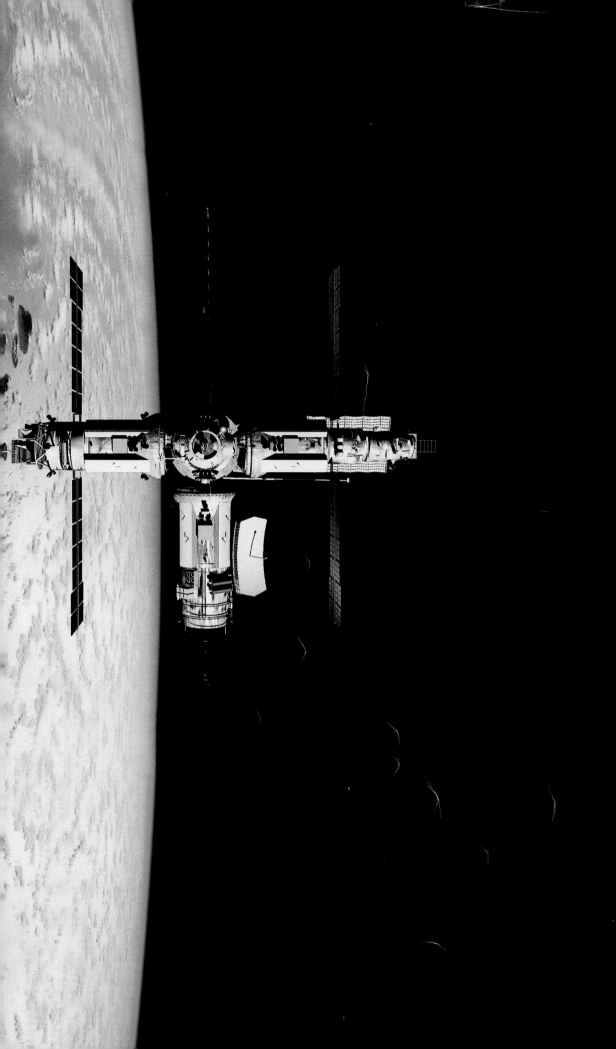

AFTER BIDDING THE RUSSIAN crew members farewell, the American astronauts exited *Mir* and boarded *Discovery* ✳ Once inside, they headed to the front of the space shuttle ✳ When everyone was in place, the docking clamps were released, and the vehicles began to drift apart ✳ As a camera monitored the docking port, the space separating the shuttle and the Russian station grew steadily larger ✳ After four minutes, the astronauts were at a safe distance from the station, and a nudge on the controls sent them into a different orbit ✳ *Mir* became smaller and smaller in the camera's image until it was out of sight on the other side of the earth ✳

Improving
Space Transport

America's space shuttle program began shortly after astronauts first set foot on the moon. In September 1969, President Richard Nixon assigned a select group of experts in the field of space technology to serve on a panel called the Space Task Group. The group's role was to advise the president on how the United States should conduct its space research and exploration program in the future.

After studying the country's space exploration situation, the Space Task Group recommended a completely new type of transportation system. In 1970, the National Aeronautics and Space Administration (NASA) began researching the design and cost of building a reusable, manned spacecraft. As engineers worked on the design, the new vehicle began to look more and more like an airplane. NASA engineers eventually started calling it a space shuttle, since it would shuttle people and materials between Earth and destinations in space.

Scientists believed that the space shuttle would be safer for human passengers than were previous manned space vehicles. It would use a safer kind of fuel than manned

The shuttle Discovery *is rolled into the Vehicle Assembly Building after a mission.*

rockets had used in the past. Studies showed that the shuttle would also be less expensive to operate, because it could fly into space over and over again with few repairs or adjustments. If necessary, NASA could launch a shuttle back into space just a few weeks after its return to Earth.

In January 1972, President Nixon announced that the U.S. government had approved NASA's plans for the space shuttle program. Later that year, NASA awarded building contracts for the new Space Transportation System (STS). Teams of workers all over the country began building the shuttle piece by piece. The shuttle's **orbiter** and its three main engines were built in California, motors for the shuttle's rocket boosters were assembled in Utah, and the shuttle's **external tank** was constructed in Louisiana.

Finally, the individual sections of the shuttle were shipped to one location for assembly and equipment testing. In September 1976, NASA announced the completion of the world's first space shuttle.

*An **orbiter** is a spacecraft designed to orbit a moon or planet.*

*An **external tank** holds the fuel needed for an orbiter's main engine.*

Once prepared for spaceflight, Columbia is rolled to the launch pad.

A
New Design

The entire space shuttle system is made up of three large and very heavy components: the orbiter, external tank, and two **solid rocket boosters**. These parts can weigh as much as 4.5 million pounds (2,025,000 kg) at launch time.

The orbiter is the part of a shuttle that resembles an airplane, both in shape and in aluminum construction. The basic shuttle design creates an orbiter 121 feet (37 m) long and 57 feet (17 m) high, with a wingspan of 78 feet (24 m). Altogether, it is about the same size as a DC-9 airliner. The orbiter, which weighs more than 160,000 pounds (67,500 kg), can carry a **payload** as heavy as 65,000 pounds (29,250 kg) into space.

Shuttle crew members spend most of their time in the forward fuselage, a compartment in the nose of the orbiter that contains the operating controls. At times, crew members may have to enter the cargo bay—an area at the back of the orbiter—to work or get supplies. The cargo bay is 60 feet (18 m) long and 15 feet (4.5 m) wide. If crew members need to take **space walks**, they can open the doors of the cargo bay while the shuttle is in orbit and step into space.

The shuttle's three main engines, located on the rear of the orbiter, launch the shuttle and make sure that it achieves the proper orbit above Earth. These extremely powerful engines, fueled by a mixture of liquid oxygen

A photograph of Atlantis from the space station Mir.

- **Solid rocket boosters** *are the two rockets attached to a shuttle's external tank.*

- *A **payload** is the cargo carried by a spacecraft.*

- *A **space walk** is a period of activity outside of an orbiting spacecraft.*

and liquid hydrogen, give the shuttle its upward **thrust**. The engines are movable, allowing the orbiter to change direction and maneuver into the proper orbit. Engines operate for just eight and a half minutes during each flight, and each engine must be replaced after it has been used for a total of seven and a half hours.

During launch, the orbiter rides piggyback on the external tank. This huge tank is 154 feet (47 m) long and 29 feet (9 m) wide. It contains the fuel for the orbiter's main engines, holding 669,186 gallons (3,042,119 L) of liquid oxygen and hydrogen. Each kind of fuel is stored in a separate compartment within the tank.

The solid rocket boosters are the third large component of the shuttle system. The two 160-foot (49 m) boosters are attached to opposite sides of the external tank. These boosters contain the largest solid **propellant** motors ever built. Each one is 116 feet (35 m) long and 12 feet (3.6 m) wide. As their name implies, they run on a solid propellant called PBAN, a fuel that looks and feels like a hard rubber eraser. Although PBAN burns at a temperature of 5,800 degrees Fahrenheit (3,204 degrees C), it is considered much safer to use than liquid fuels.

Endeavour *is attached to the external tank and solid rocket boosters (left);* Columbia *launching skyward (right).*

Although the solid rocket boosters run only during the first two minutes of a launch, their power—together with that of the main engines—gives the shuttle enough thrust to reach its orbit. When the shuttle reaches an altitude of 24 miles (39 km) above Earth, the boosters separate from the external tank. They then fall on parachutes into the Atlantic Ocean, where they are recovered by a waiting ship and returned to land. NASA workers then prepare them for use on another flight.

A **propellant** *is a fuel that drives, or pushes, an object forward.*

Thrust *is the pushing force generated by a rocket engine.*

The
Shuttle Fleet

The U.S. government initially had planned to name the first space shuttle *Constitution,* in honor of the country's 1976 bicentennial. But fans of the 1960s television show "Star Trek" started a letter-writing campaign, urging President Nixon to name the shuttle *Enterprise,* after the huge spaceship in the popular television series. Their campaign worked, and the shuttle was christened *Enterprise.* Around NASA, though, the orbiters' official names are a bit duller. *Enterprise*'s orbiter, for example, is OV-101, which stands for Orbiter Vehicle-101.

Although shuttles are designed to orbit the earth, *Enterprise* was only a test vehicle that was never equipped to fly in space. NASA put *Enterprise*'s components through hundreds of tests to make sure that the system could survive the extreme stress of launch, flight, and landing.

During 1977, NASA subjected *Enterprise* to 13 ALTs, or Approach and Landing Tests. The tests were divided into three phases. Phase one consisted of five "captive" flights. For these tests, NASA mounted the orbiter on top of a special Boeing 747 jumbo jet known as the shuttle carrier aircraft (SCA). As the unmanned *Enterprise* rode piggyback into the air, SCA pilots and crews on the ground tested the orbiter's wind resistance, mechanical systems, and maneuverability in the air.

For the three phase two flights, NASA again mounted the orbiter on the SCA. This time, however, the orbiter carried a crew of two men, who controlled the vehicle's flight while monitoring all systems.

Before liftoff, each shuttle travels 3.5 miles (5.6 km) to the launch pad.

During the five phase-three flights, the SCA flew to a high altitude before releasing *Enterprise*. The orbiter then glided through the air and landed gently on a runway; crew members riding inside the orbiter tested its landing capabilities. *Enterprise* performed very well on all tests, generating a lot of optimism for the future of America's space program.

Although *Enterprise* never made it into space, NASA has used it many times to train shuttle crews. The shuttle has also appeared in air shows all over the world. In 1984, the orbiter traveled by barge to New Orleans, Louisiana, where it was exhibited during the World's Fair.

Enterprise left the Kennedy Space Center for the last time in November 1985. The SCA flew the historic spacecraft to Washington, D.C., where *Enterprise* became the property of the Smithsonian Institution.

NASA soon commissioned five more shuttles, all named after famous sailing ships. The oldest orbiter in the shuttle fleet is *Columbia*, which is named after a ship from the 1700s. Other famous vessels have also carried the name *Columbia*, including the first U.S. Navy ship to circle the earth and the command **module** of the first lunar landing mission.

A **module** is a part of a spacecraft that can be detached and operated by itself.

Endeavour *arrives at the Kennedy Space Center on top of the SCA (top); a drag chute helps landing shuttles stop (bottom).*

In April 1981, *Columbia* made history by becoming the first shuttle ever launched into space. NASA called the mission STS-1, or Space Transportation System 1. Although it was a risky mission for pilots Robert Crippen and John Young—who were flying in a shuttle system that had never been tested in space—the astronauts encountered no problems. NASA's first shuttle mission was a success.

NASA launched the second orbiter, *Challenger*, for the first time in July 1982. This shuttle was named after an American naval research ship that sailed the Atlantic and Pacific Oceans during the 1870s. The *Apollo 17* lunar module also carried this name.

Challenger completed only nine missions during four years of duty. The shuttle's 10th mission ended in tragedy on the morning of January 28, 1986. Just 73 seconds after takeoff, the **O rings** on one of the solid rocket boosters failed, causing the orbiter to disintegrate in a giant ball of fire that killed all seven crew members. The area where the crew sat was blown away from the orbiter and fell

O rings *are rubber rings that seal a joint on a solid rocket booster.*

Astronaut John Glenn made history in 1998 and 1962 (top);
images of the Challenger disaster (bottom).

46,000 feet (14,020 m) before crashing into the Atlantic Ocean. The *Challenger* explosion was the worst disaster in NASA history.

The third shuttle, called *Discovery*, is one of NASA's lighter shuttles. It weighs in at 171,000 pounds (76,950 kg), 6,970 pounds (3,091 kg) lighter than *Columbia*. In October 1998, *Discovery* carried John Glenn—the first

American to orbit the earth—back into space 36 years after his historic voyage.

Atlantis became the fourth member of the orbiter fleet
in 1985. Because builders now had considerable experi-
ence in constructing orbiters, they were able to assemble
Atlantis in only four years—almost half the time it took to
build Columbia. One of Atlantis's most famous missions
took place in 1989, when the shuttle carried a spacecraft
called Galileo into space. Atlantis then released Galileo,
which went on to explore planets in our solar system.

Endeavour, the youngest shuttle in NASA's fleet, was

The Galileo *spacecraft is released from* Atlantis's *cargo bay.*

A **drag chute** *is a large parachute that helps to slow an orbiter during its landing.*

built as a replacement for *Challenger*. Its name—the winning suggestion in a national contest among elementary and middle school students—came once again from a famous ship of the 1700s.

Included in *Endeavour* were many new or improved features. These features have performed so well that NASA has added them to the other three shuttles. The upgrades included a 40-foot (12 m) wide **drag chute**, better computers, and improved braking systems. NASA has also improved the plumbing and electrical systems of the shuttles, allowing orbiters to stay in space for up to 28 days.

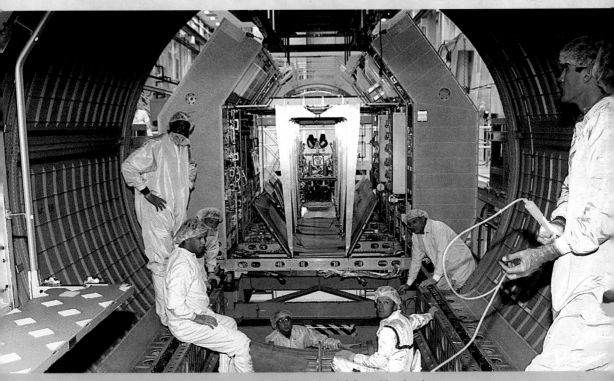

Space station technicians install a payload delivered by shuttle.

Linking Earth and Space

All space shuttles leave the earth and return to it in the same way. NASA workers connect the orbiter, the external tank, and the solid rocket boosters. They fill the tanks with fuel. Then they move the shuttle to one of two launch pads at the Kennedy Space Center in Florida.

The shuttle sits on the launch pad until its **launch window** opens. NASA is not always able to launch a shuttle during a particular launch window. Tests may reveal a problem with one of the shuttle's components, or weather conditions—storms, high winds, cloud cover, or cold temperatures—may prevent a shuttle's launch.

When launch time arrives and all systems and conditions are "go," the orbiter's main engines and solid rocket boosters fire at the same time, lifting the heavy shuttle and its crew off the launch pad with a deafening roar. Two minutes into the flight, the rocket boosters shut down and detach from the external tank. They then drift on parachutes into the Atlantic Ocean.

The orbiter's main engines operate for several more minutes until the shuttle has almost reached orbit. As the

A breathtaking look at the 2,250-ton (2,040 t) shuttle system launching from Earth.

shuttle nears its orbit, the external tank runs out of fuel. It then detaches from the orbiter and falls through the earth's atmosphere. Because the tank has no parachutes or protective covering, it burns up and breaks into small pieces that land in the ocean.

The shuttle pilot fires small rocket thrusters to steer the shuttle into its orbit. The altitude of the orbit depends on the nature of the mission. It can be as low as 155 miles (249 km) above the earth or as high as 600 miles (966

The **launch window** *is a period of time during which a launch must occur.*

Discovery crew members place the Hubble Space Telescope *in orbit.*

km). While in orbit, the shuttle races around the earth at about 17,500 miles (28,175 km) per hour. At this speed, it completely circles the planet in 90 minutes. This means that crew members see a sunrise or sunset every 45 minutes.

After the shuttle achieves its orbit, crew members start their mission. They may have to release a **satellite** or repair one that is already in orbit. The mission may involve docking the shuttle with the Russian space station *Mir*. Other shuttle missions may involve secret military projects or scientific experiments using plants, medicine, or animals.

An average mission lasts about 10 days, but the crew carries enough supplies to stay in orbit longer in case weather

A shuttle appears to be upside down while in orbit around the earth.

*A **satellite** is an object—natural or man-made—that orbits a celestial body.*

__Heat shielding tiles__ are special insulating tiles that protect an orbiter from intense heat.

conditions or technical problems delay the shuttle's return. The crew generally consists of six to eight people, but shuttles can hold up to 10 astronauts.

When it's time to come back to Earth, the pilot again fires thrusters to gently nudge the shuttle out of orbit and back into the earth's atmosphere. Special **heat shielding tiles** cover the outside of the shuttle. These tiles prevent

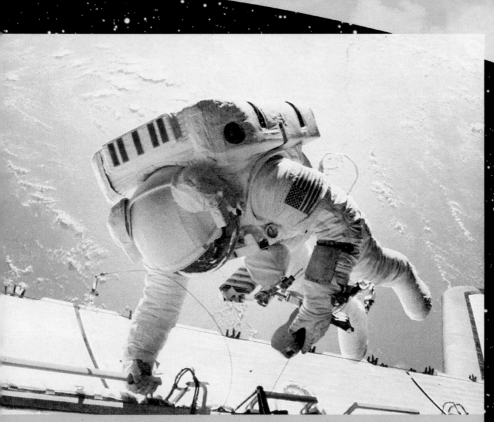

A space walk can be dangerous even though astronauts are tethered to the shuttle.

JUNE 27, 1995

Atlantis *docks for the first time with the Russian space station* Mir.

the friction of reentering the atmosphere from burning up the shuttle. Gravity soon takes hold of the shuttle, and the pilot lands by steering the gliding orbiter toward a runway.

Most of the time, shuttles land at the Kennedy Space Center. However, if the weather there is poor, the pilot may have to land on a dry lake bed at Edwards Air Force Base in California. When the shuttle comes down at Edwards, the SCA must transport the orbiter back to Kennedy. Each trip back to Florida aboard the SCA costs about a million dollars, so NASA tries to land shuttles in Florida whenever possible.

As its wheels touch down on the runway, the shuttle is traveling between 205 and 235 miles (330 to 378 km) per hour. A drag chute pops out from the back to help the shuttle's brakes slow the orbiter.

When the shuttle comes to a stop, the mission has officially ended. NASA specialists then inspect the vehicle. They check engines, remove any leftover fuel, and ventilate the cargo bay to dispel any accumulated gases. The inspection can take as long as an hour, but crew members must remain inside until it has been completed. While they're waiting, crew members shut down each of the shuttle's operating systems.

A rear view of Discovery landing (top);
shuttles are thoroughly inspected after every mission (bottom).

Blazing Onward

The space shuttle program has been the most useful and versatile one in the history of space exploration. Shuttle crews have launched and repaired the satellites that make global communication and television coverage possible. One shuttle mission placed the *Hubble Space Telescope* in orbit. This huge telescope lets scientists study the universe without having to look through Earth's thick atmosphere. A later shuttle mission repaired a mirror in the telescope.

Shuttle crews have conducted hundreds of low-cost scientific experiments in space. Some of these experiments have tested medicines in a weightless environment. Because medicines sometimes work differently in gravity-free conditions, shuttle experiments could lead to new ways of treating diseases.

In 1998, the U.S., Canada, and 14 other nations began working together on a spacecraft called the International Space Station. When finished, the space station will become a long-term "home" in space for astronauts, scientists, and other people. The space shuttle system will play

The massive Hubble Space Telescope *is carefully released into orbit from* Endeavour *after repairs.*

a big role in this project. Shuttle crews will place the station's modules into orbit, then put them together in space. Later, shuttles will be used to transport people and supplies to the space station.

Several nations have also begun working together to develop a new type of shuttle called an aerospace plane. This vehicle promises to be even safer and less expensive than the current shuttles. Instead of launching vertically like a rocket, the aerospace plane will take off and land horizontally, like an airplane. It will also be able to take off from an airborne carrier plane, just as airplanes at sea can take off from aircraft carriers. This aerospace plane may well become the space shuttle system of the future.

Since its birth in the 1970s, the space shuttle system has been NASA's most versatile and frequent means of space transportation. In fact, the shuttle's orbiter has become NASA's most recognizable symbol. Although the aerospace plane may replace it in the future, the shuttle has become the definitive spacecraft of the 20th century.

The future of space shuttle vehicles: the X-30 Aerospace Plane.

INDEX